Happy, Sad, Jealous, Mad

Stories, Rhymes, and Activities that Help Children Understand their Emotions

by
Jo Browning-Wroe

illustrated by
Julie Anderson

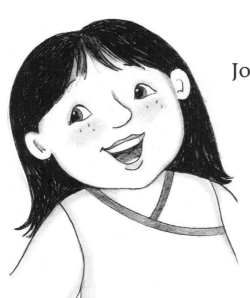

Key Education
An imprint of Carson-Dellosa Publishing LLC
Greensboro, North Carolina
www.keyeducationpublishing.com

~~~~~~

CONGRATULATIONS ON YOUR PURCHASE OF A KEY EDUCATION PRODUCT!

The editors at Key Education are former teachers who bring experience, enthusiasm, and quality to each and every product. Thousands of teachers have looked to the staff at Key Education for new and innovative resources to make their work more enjoyable and rewarding. Key Education is committed to developing and publishing educational materials that will assist teachers in building a strong and developmentally appropriate curriculum for young children.

PLAN FOR GREAT TEACHING EXPERIENCES WHEN YOU USE EDUCATIONAL MATERIALS FROM KEY EDUCATION PUBLISHING

~~~~~~

Credits
Author: Jo Browning-Wroe
Publisher: Sherrill B. Flora
Creative Director: Annette Hollister-Papp
Cover Design: Annette Hollister-Papp
Inside Illustrations: Julie Anderson
Editor: George C. Flora
Production: Key Education Staff

About the Author:

Jo Browning Wroe has taught both in the United Kingdom and in the United States. She earned her undergraduate degrees in English and Education from Cambridge University, Cambridge, England. She worked for twelve years in educational publishing before completing a Masters Degree in Creative Writing from the University of East Anglia, Norwich, England. Most of her time is now spent writing teacher resource materials and running workshops for others who love to write. Jo has been the recipient of the National Toy Libraries Award. She lives in Cambridge, England with her two daughters, Alice and Ruby, and her husband, John.

Key Education

An imprint of Carson-Dellosa Publishing LLC
PO Box 35665
Greensboro, NC 27425 USA
www.keyeducationpublishing.com

ISBN 1-933052-73-2
01-325118091

Contents

Introduction

Even young children express strong emotions. Only an adult who does not know any children, or hasn't any memory of being a child, would argue that this is not true. It is surprising then, that we do not do more to help our children understand and learn more about their emotions.

Included in each chapter of *Happy, Sad, Jealous, Mad* the teacher will find the following:

- A teacher's guide page filled with suggestions, activities, and guided questions.

- Each teacher's page is followed by a delightful story where the children learn about Clara Clapton and her adorable dog, Bumper. Clara is a six year old girl who has moved from Chicago to Richmond, Virginia. She misses her friends, her apartment, and does not find it easy to settle into her new school and neighborhood. Her closest companion is her puppy, Bumper. Each night, Clara confides in Bumper and tells him all the adventures of her day and the feelings that she has experienced.

  Clara's stories seek to demonstrate that an integral part of being human is to experience a wide range of emotions, some of which can be uncomfortable and unpleasant. By becoming familiar with the vocabulary, and the facial and bodily expressions of those feelings, young children can become more empathetic to others and more understanding of their own emotional lives. The stories are reproducible and designed in booklet form so they may be copied and sent home for the children to share and discuss with their parents.

- A "Letter to Parents" is included on page 5. Send this letter home before you begin sharing the stories and activities with the children. This letter will encourage the parents to look for, and read again, the stories that the children will be bringing home.

- Emotion picture cards of Clara and Bumper accompany each story. These cards can be reproduced and used as discussion starters before the story is read, or as a springboard for comprehension questions.

- A fun poem about the highlighted emotion is included in each chapter. Each poem comes with some type of special activity: memorize it as a class; create puppets; and act-it-out are just a few examples.

- Each chapter concludes with several reproducible student pages that allow the children to further explore the emotion through engaging and targeted activities.

As the teacher, you may wish to work through the entire book in chronological order, although each story has been written in a way that allows you to pick and choose the stories in any sequence—the chapters do stand alone.

Finally, when encouraging children to talk about emotions, it is possible that someone might make some sort of disclosure during class. Ensure that you are fully conversant with your school's child protection procedures so you can be confident of what course to follow should that happen.

Letter To Parents

Dear Parents,

Our class will be working on an instructional unit on "Emotions" and "Feelings." The children will be bringing home seven delightful stories, each story featuring a six year old girl named Clara Clapton and her adorable dog, Bumper. Clara has moved from Chicago to Richmond, Virginia. She misses her friends, her apartment, and does not find it easy to settle into her new school and neighborhood. Her closest companion is her puppy, Bumper. Each night *(and in each story)*, Clara confides in Bumper and tells him all about the adventures of her day and the feelings that she has experienced.

Clara's stories seek to demonstrate that an integral part of being human is to experience a wide range of emotions. By becoming familiar with the vocabulary, and the facial and bodily expressions of those feelings, young children can learn to become more empathetic towards others and gain more understanding of their own feelings.

The children will be bringing these adorable stories home to share and discuss with you. Enjoy reading them together!

Sincerely,

_____

Your child's teacher

- -

Directions for Preparing Materials

The Story Booklets

Student Story Booklets: Copy, cut out each page, and staple them together in alphabetical order. The finished booklets will be approximately 5 x 7.5 inches.

Classroom Story Booklets: Enlarge each page to fit on an 11 x 17 inch piece of paper. Cut out each page and staple them together in alphabetical order. The illustrations may be colored or left black and white. Enlarging the pages will ensure that when you read the story to a group of children that they will be able to clearly see the illustrations.

Emotion Picture Cards

Copy onto card stock, color, cut out, and laminate the emotion picture cards for durability. Save and display them on a bulletin board after each story.

Character Patterns on pages 91-94 and Scenery Patterns on pages 95-96

Stick Puppets: Copy, color, cut out the patterns, and laminate them for durability. Attach the pattern to a craft stick or tongue depressor by using double-sided tape. To create larger stick puppets, simply enlarge the patterns on a photocopy machine and finish as directed above. Attach the laminated patterns to paint stir sticks, 12 inch rulers, or wooden spoons.

String Puppets: Copy, color, cut out the patterns, and laminate them for durability. Fold a 3" x 5" index card in half lengthwise. Place a 24" piece of yarn or string along the fold and tape the card closed. Tape the two ends of the string to the back top of the pattern. The card is now a handle that the children can use to manipulate the string puppet. These string puppets have nice movement and are easy for small hands to manipulate.

Flannel Board or Magnetic Board Patterns: Copy, color, cut out the patterns, and laminate them for durability. For use on a flannel board, glue sandpaper or felt to the back of each pattern piece, or use self-stick Velcro®. For use on a magnetic board, attach a small piece of self-stick magnetic tape (found at most craft or hardware stores) on the back of each pattern.

Scenery Patterns: Follow the same directions for the flannel board character patterns. Place the scenery on the flannel board and use as the backdrop for a puppet show.

How Do You Feel?

Directions: This activity can be used with any of the stories in *Happy, Sad, Jealous, Mad*. Have the children draw the emotion from the story on the face below or have each child draw the facial features that show how they are feeling.

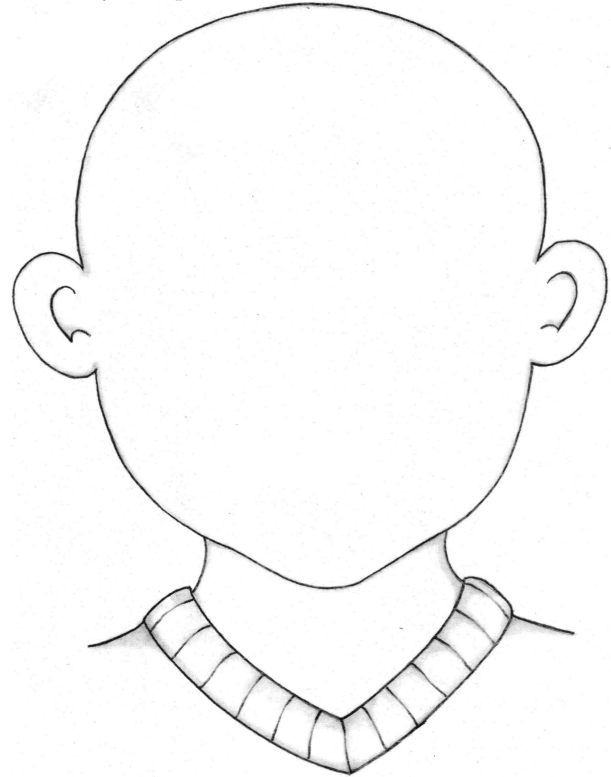

Chapter One: Teacher's Guide
An Introduction to Emotions

A. Before The Story

1. **We are Going to Learn About Emotions**. Explain to the children that they will be learning about emotions/feelings. Ask the children to share their own definitions of what they believe emotions/feelings are. Brainstorm a list of emotions/feelings words.

2. **What Do Feelings Look Like?** Use a hand mirror and ask the children to look at themselves as they make various facial expressions. Discuss that you can often "see" how someone feels just by looking at their face.

B. Read The Story

Reproduce the **Read-to-Me Story 1: *Clara and Bumper*** found on pages 8–14. Make the storybooks according to the directions on page 5. Read the story to the children. Stop and discuss each page and let the children enjoy getting to know Clara and Bumper. To retell the story as a visual presentation, prepare the character and scenery patterns found on pages 91 through 96. Directions for making the patterns are also found on page 5.

C. After The Story

Comprehension Questions:
1. Name some of the different emotions that Clara feels in this chapter *(loneliness, love for Bumper, excitement, joy, embarrassment)*.
2. How was Clara's new home different from her old one?
3. What were some of the things Clara did to behave like a dog?
4. What did Clara's mom suggest that Clara do, instead of behaving like a dog?
5. What did Bumper do to make Clara think he wanted to know what it is like to be human?
6. Prepare the **Emotion Picture Cards** found on pages 15–16 according to the directions on page 5. Show the cards to the children and discuss the cards. Each card represents a section of the story and an emotion felt by Clara or Bumper.

Discussion Time
1. Why can it be hard to start at a new school?
2. How could you make it easier for a new person in the class?
3. Have any of you felt any of the emotions that Clara had in this chapter?

D. Extension Activities

1. **Poem**. Teach the poem "Feelings" found on page 17. Copy a set of the stick puppets on page 17 for each child. Have the children color, cut out, and attach each puppet to a craft stick by using double-stick tape. The puppets can be held up at the appropriate sections when reciting the poem.
2. **Matching Faces**. Reproduce page 18 and follow the directions.
3. **Cut and Paste a Face**. Reproduce page 19 and follow the directions.

Read-to-Me Story 1

Clara and Bumper

"Clara Clapton, get up off your hands and knees, and walk on two legs like a human being!"

"I'm not a human being. I'm a dog, like Bumper," said Clara as she crawled out into the backyard and snuggled up to the puppy that was asleep in the sun. Clara's mother and father were left in the kitchen on their own.

Chapter 1: Clara and Bumper -A-

"I don't know what to do," said Clara's mother, "Ever since we've had Bumper she's been behaving like a dog. She carries her backpack in her mouth, drinks water from a bowl, and scratches her ear with her foot!"

"I think we should leave her alone," said her father. "Moving to a new house and starting at a new school has been tough. Bumper's her only friend at the moment. Don't worry, I'm sure she will soon grow out of it."

They looked out through the open kitchen door, where their 6-year old daughter was curled up next to Bumper on the warm deck.

Chapter 1: Clara and Bumper -B-

Her new home in Richmond was very different. It was a house, on a quiet street, with lots of tall trees. All the houses had large yards. It was a pretty neighborhood, but there was too much space and not enough children to fill it. Clara was the only girl on her block. She missed knowing that Beth was above her and that Denna was below her. She was lonely.

"I'm pleased she loves the puppy," Clara's mom replied, "I just wish she didn't want to be one. It's driving me crazy. Did you know she's stopped using towels after a shower? She shakes herself dry, like Bumper! Like Bumper, like Bumper, like Bumper, that's all Clara says."

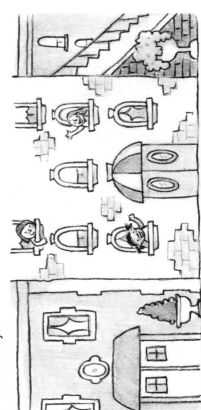

Clara's parents gave her Bumper three months ago. Her family had moved from Chicago, Illinois to Richmond, Virginia. Clara used to live in the center of a big city, in a beautiful old apartment building. Her two best friends lived in the same building. Beth lived on the floor above Clara and Denna on the floor below Clara. The three girls were always playing together in each other's apartments.

"A puppy!" There were tears in Clara's eyes, which was odd, she thought, because she was so happy.

The puppy scrambled out of the box, and his paws clicked on the surface of the table. His tail wagged and bumped against the box, knocking it on to the floor. Clara picked up the wiggling puppy and brushed her cheek against his soft, golden fur.

From that day, the only time Clara and Bumper were apart was when she had to be at school. Each morning, Bumper stood by the back door, whining, looking from Clara to the door, and back to Clara again.

So one afternoon, Clara's dad came home early from work carrying a huge box. When he put the box on the kitchen table, Clara was a little scared to see that the box moved all on its own.

"Quick, Clara! Open it, before it falls off!" Her parents were laughing, so she figured that whatever was in the box wasn't going to hurt her. She walked towards the bouncing box, pulled up the cardboard flaps, and a furry face burst out and licked her nose.

They did everything together. They watched TV lying on the Oriental rug in the den. They played with a ball in the backyard. Bumper sat under the table when Clara ate her dinner, and she sat on the floor next to him when he ate his.

At bedtime Clara was tucked into bed by her parents, and as soon as they had said good-night and closed the door, she patted her bedspread. Immediately, Bumper would jump out of his basket and scramble up onto the bed.

"I want to take you with me Bumper, but I can't. Teachers do not allow dogs in school – silly people," Clara said, kneeling down to cuddle him goodbye.

Once the door clicked shut, Bumper would sigh, lie down, and spend the day waiting for Clara to come home. At 3:30 when the car pulled up in the driveway, he would run round the kitchen, yelping and barking until Clara came through the door. Then he would jump up and down, sliding his big paws down her legs.

And when Clara ran up to the mailman on Saturday morning, growling and snarling until he dropped his letters, her Mom said nothing.

But then on Sunday night, Clara did something that made even her father agree that the time had come to say something, and Clara's doggy behavior had to stop. It was bedtime. The evening air was warm so the back door was still open. Clara's dad was loading the dishwasher. He could hear the chirping of the crickets outside. Every now and then the glow of a firefly flashed in the dark.

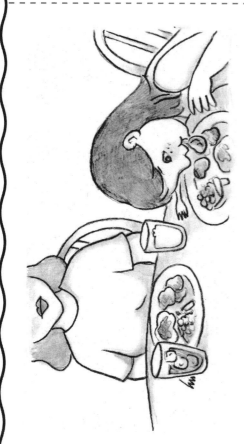

Clara's mom could see how much Clara and Bumper loved each other, so she decided to try and ignore her daughter's strange behavior. At dinner that night, when Clara picked her chicken up off the plate with her teeth, her Mom said nothing.

When Clara gave her mother's face a lick, instead of a kiss goodbye the next morning, her mom said nothing.

In an angry whisper, so the neighbors wouldn't hear, Clara's father said "Get inside! Right now!"

"There are some things that little girls must not do!" he said. Once they were in the kitchen with the door closed, he continued saying, "and using a tree as a bathroom is one of those things!

"Bumper does. Why can't I?" Clara didn't seem sorry at all.

Chapter 1: Clara and Bumper -L-

Clara's mom came in to the kitchen. She asked Clara's Dad, "Have you seen Clara?"

"No, I thought she was getting ready for bed," he replied.

"So did I, but when I went to say good-night to her she was not in her room. I heard her brushing her teeth a few minutes ago, but now she's vanished," she said.

Out of the corner of his eye, Clara's dad saw something move in the backyard and a second later he heard an excited yelp.

"I think they're in the backyard," he said, opening the screen door and going out on the deck. Clara's mother followed. The white of Clara's nightie and Bumper's golden fur almost shone in the darkness.

Clara's mother gasped, "Clara Clapton, what on earth do you think you're doing?"

Chapter 1: Clara and Bumper -K-

Clara looked down at Bumper's face resting on her knees, "Since Bumper came," her mom continued, "he's taught you a lot about dogs. Maybe now it's your turn to teach him about people."

Clara suddenly felt embarrassed about the things she had done over the last few days; growling at the mailman, carrying things in her mouth, and (most of all) using the back yard as a bathroom.

Bumper's face on her knee felt heavy and warm. His brown eyes looked so clever and kind, "Do you want to know what it's like to be human, Bumper?" she asked, stroking his velvet nose.

Bumper stood up. His tail swung from left to right, and his feet pitter- pattered on the kitchen tiles.

"I think that's a yes," said Dad.

"So do I," laughed Clara.

Clara's mother took her hand and led her to sit down at the table. Bumper went and sat under the table, leaning against Clara's legs.

"Clara, Darling," said her mom, "this has got to stop. I know you love Bumper with all your heart, but there's no need for you to behave like a dog. He already knows how dogs behave. Don't you think it would be more helpful to Bumper to teach him what it's like to be human? After all, it's humans that Bumper has to learn to live with, not dogs."

Clara feels silly.

Clara feels happy.

Clara feels lonely.

Clara feels scared.

Clara feels excited.

Bumper feels sad.

Clara's dad feels angry.

Clara feels embarrassed.

Feelings

Sometimes I'm happy, sometimes I'm lonely
Sometimes I'm worried and sad
Sometimes I'm brave, sometimes I'm scared
Sometimes I'm angry and mad.

I smile when I'm happy, I cry when I'm lonely
I shout and stamp if I'm mad
I shake when I'm scared, blush if embarrassed
And jump up and down when I'm glad.

Stick Puppet Patterns

Directions: Read the poem "Feelings" to the children and discuss each of the emotions. Copy the five children below, color, cut out, and laminate them for durability. Attach the finished patterns to craft sticks using double-stick tape. Let the children enjoy using the stick puppets as you read the poem.

Matching Faces

Directions: Draw a line and match the identical faces.

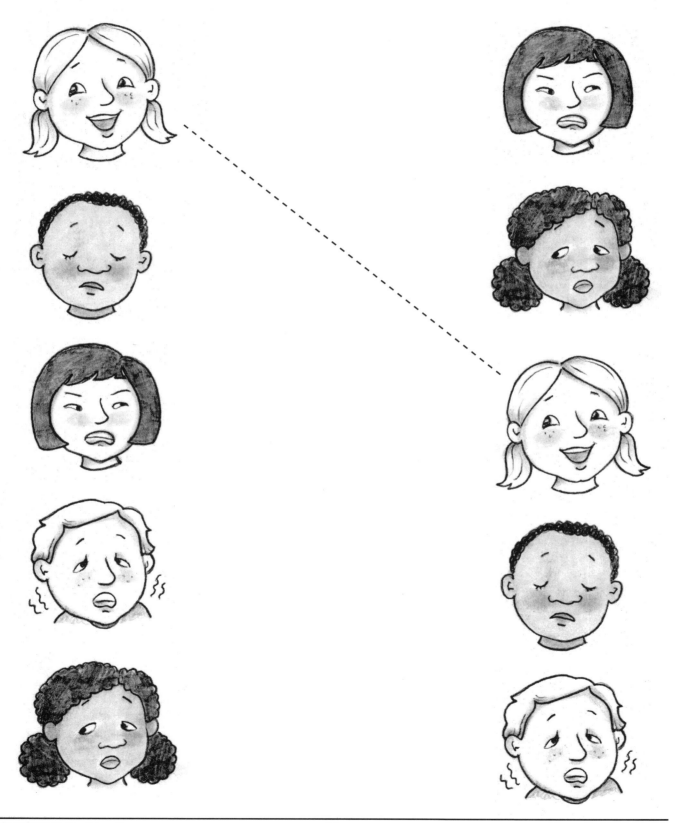

Cut and Paste a Face

Directions: Cut and paste the features to make a happy, sad, or angry face.

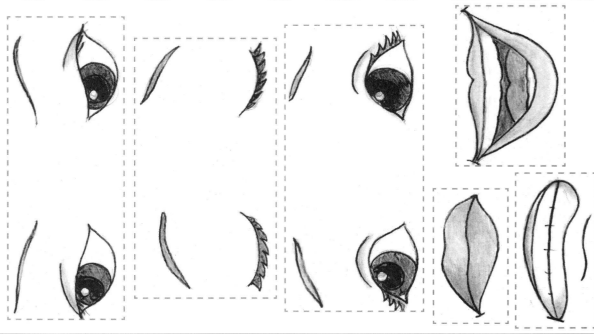

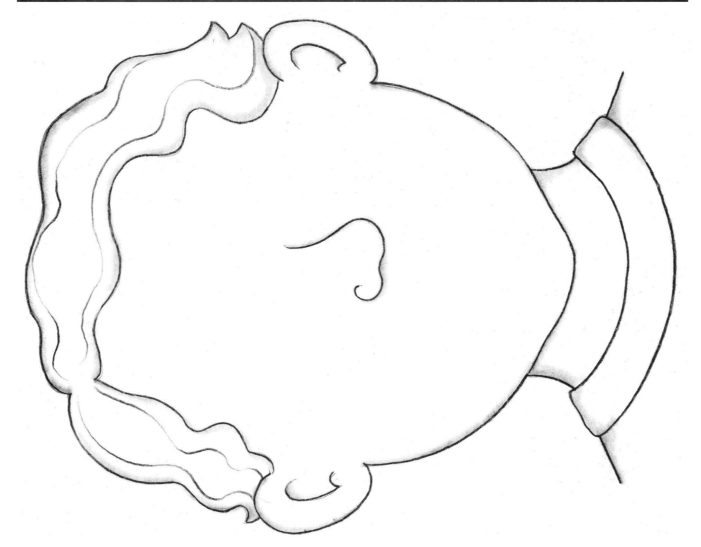

 Happy, Sad, Jealous, Mad

Chapter Two: Teacher's Guide
The Emotion: Scared

A. Before The Story

Prepare the **Emotion Picture Cards** found on page 28 according to the directions on page 5. Show the cards to the children and discuss how Clara and Bumper are feeling. Here are some guided questions:

1. How do you think Clara and Bumper are feeling in these pictures?
2. How can you tell they are scared?
3. What kinds of things scare you? What do you do when you are scared?
4. What do you think has happened that is making Clara and Bumper feel scared? Let's read the story and find out!

B. Read The Story

Reproduce the **Read-to-Me Story 2: Scared** found on pages 21–27. Make the storybooks according to the directions on page 5. Read the story to the children. Stop and discuss each page. Let the children ask questions and try to predict what might happen next. To retell the story as a visual presentation, prepare the character and scenery patterns found on pages 91 through 96. Directions for making the patterns are found on page 5.

C. After The Story

Comprehension Questions:

1. What did Bumper do that Clara wanted to try and copy?
2. Why did she stop herself from doing it?
3. What is the one thing that Clara likes about school?
4. What were the 'weird' things that happened to Clara's body when she was scared?
5. Who was kind to Clara in this chapter?

Discussion Time

1. What happens to your body when you get scared?
2. Discuss the differences between being scared of imaginary things rather than genuinely dangerous situations.
3. What are some of the things we can do to stop being scared of imaginary things? *(Some examples: talk to an adult or a friend, cuddle a toy, listen to a story on tape, or music.)*

D. Extension Activities

1. **Poem**. Teach the poem "Scared" found on page 29. Copy the movable puppet patterns found on page 29 onto card stock for each child. Have the children color, cut out, and attach the puppet's arms and legs with brads. The puppet's arms and legs can be moved to make the puppet look scared.
2. **When Something Scares You – What Should You Do?** Reproduce page 30 and follow the directions.
3. **What's Behind the Door?** Reproduce page 31 and follow the directions.

Read-to-Me Story 2

Scared

"Sleep well Clara."

"Good night Mom," Clara pretended to look sleepy. Her mom asked, "Shall I leave the door open?"

"No thanks," Clara closed her eyes, waiting for the door to click shut.

As soon as her mother's footsteps reached the bottom of the stairs, Clara sat up in bed and patted her bedspread, "Come on Bumper," she whispered.

Immediately, the soft, wiggly body of Clara's puppy leapt from his basket and onto her bed. He sniffed and grunted in excitement as he licked her face. Then Bumper turned around and around on the spot three times before settling down. He curled his body into a little ball, his tail wrapping over the tip of his nose.

Clara wondered if she could lie in a little ball like Bumper. She was about to try, when she remembered the promise she had made to her mom. She laid back down and put her hand on Bumper's head.

"I nearly forgot Bumper. I'm going to try and not behave like a dog anymore. It gets me into trouble. I'm going to tell you about being a human instead," said Clara.

Bumper lifted his head and looked at Clara as if he understood every word she said.

There's not much that I like about school. The only girl who talks to me is Mary-Lou Hammerton and she only talks to me because no one else likes her. I want to be friends with Harriet Lewis, Jessica Rickman, and Christie Micks. They are the most popular girls in the class. They have the best clothes and they always play the best games together at recess. The problem is that they don't seem to want to be friends with me.

Most of the time I'm on my own, and if Mary-Lou Hammerton comes up to me I just smile because I don't have much to say. Eventually, she walks away and I am alone again. Mary-Lou gave me some of her snack the other day.

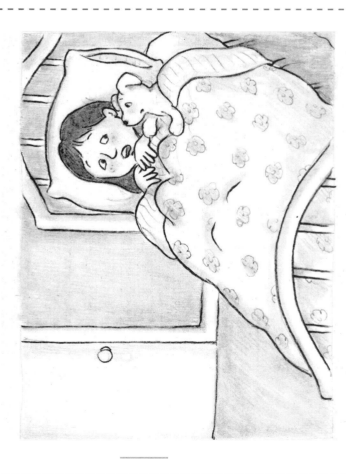

"It's not easy being a human," she said, her face in front of his. "So, because you are my best friend, it's probably a good idea if you try and understand just how hard it is sometimes."

Bumper sighed, and put his head on Clara's lap.

"Sometimes, it can be scary," said Clara.

Bumper lifted his head and raised his eyebrows. He seemed particularly interested to hear about the scariness.

"I'll tell you all about it Bumper, but I'll have to whisper. Mom thinks we're asleep."

Bumper uncurled himself and sat up to watch Clara plump up her pillows.

He didn't take his eyes off the girl with the big blue eyes and long dark hair as she told him her story.

Monday morning is the only time I look forward to these days because we play soccer for an hour. When I lived in Chicago, I played in a team on Saturday mornings, so I know I'm the best, by far. Kids even fight over me when the teams are picked. Today it was very hot and lots of people didn't have the energy to try very hard. I did though, and by the end of the game, I had scored 5 goals! Our team won 7 goals to 2. I was sweaty and thirsty, but I felt great, and Jessica Rickman said "Clara, well done!"

So school really isn't much fun, and I'm not especially good at math or reading. I'm not bad, but I don't get the best grades. There is only one thing I like about school. It's the one thing that I'm really good at — soccer. I can say this to you Bumper and you won't think that I'm showing off, but I can run faster, jump higher, and kick balls better than any kid in my class.

Mrs. Grover, my teacher, asked me to take the bag of soccer balls back to the equipment room. It's a tiny little room, next to our classroom, and it has no windows and it's stuffed full of things – soccer balls, basketballs, and bowling equipment. If you are in there it's important to prop the door open with your foot, because sometimes it closes and locks itself. There's no light in there either, so you can only see when the door is open.

I needed to hang the bag of balls over a hook on the back wall. I thought if I did it really quickly, I could take my foot from the door and get back again before it closed. I was wrong. The door swung shut, and everything went completely black. I mean completely black. I couldn't see my hand in front of me. I was locked in. On my own.

Bumper, after today I know all about being scared, and let me tell you, when you get scared weird things happen to your body. I don't know what dog-scared feels like, but this is what human-scared felt like to me. The first thing is you find out exactly where your heart is. Normally it beats away without you noticing, but when you're scared, it thumps against your ribs, and makes you feel like you're out of breath. Other parts of your body seem to thump along with your heart too, like inside your ears.

And another thing, your mouth goes all dry. The dentist has a little machine that he puts in your mouth when you get a filling, to suck up all the wet. It stops you needing to swallow. When you're really scared, it feels like you've got one of those machines in your mouth.

It seemed that it took forever for anyone to come, because I was all on my own and in the dark. When the first footsteps walked passed, I knocked quietly and said, "Hello? Please can someone let me out?"

That's when I discovered that your voice can go all wobbly too, when you're scared. They were all making so much noise in the hall that nobody heard me.

I took a deep breath, knocked my fist against the door, and then shouted at the top of my voice, "Open the door! Let me out!"

The voices stopped. The footsteps stopped. Then a boy, I think it was Matthew Knight, said, "There's someone in the equipment room."

And the last thing I noticed this morning, when I was trying to pull the door open, is that parts of my body started to wobble. My hands shook and my knees jumped up and down. It makes me sound like a cartoon character, but that really is what happened to me in the equipment room today.

After a minute, it wasn't quite so dark and I noticed a strip of light from under the door. I still couldn't really see anything, just shapes all around me. I imagined everyone else talking and laughing. I wondered if anyone had missed me. In a few moments, the class would walk past this door on their way back to the classroom. I would have to bang on the door and shout for them to let me out. I'd feel stupid as well as scared.

Suddenly, the room filled with light. My eyes scrunched themselves shut. I squinted at the open doorway and there stood Mary-Lou Hammerton.

Mary Lou said, "I heard Christie, Jessica, and Harriet laughing about you being locked in, so I came back when they weren't looking."

All I could say was, "Thanks," because I was trying so hard not to cry. I was so relieved!

"Get up and then just walk in the classroom and pretend like nothing's wrong. Don't give them the pleasure of seeing you upset."

"Thanks," was all I could say.

I scrambled out the door and ran into the classroom.

Chapter 2: Scared -L-

Then I heard a girl's voice and I know for sure whose voice I heard — it was Harriet Lewis. She said, "Clara must still be in there. Mrs. Grover chose her to put the balls away. Leave her in there a little bit longer. It serves her right for being the teacher's favorite."

The footsteps walked away. Then I got even more scared. How long would I be left in there? What if I missed lunch? What if I was still in there when it came time to go home? What if I was there all night, all by myself?

Chapter 2: Scared -K-

When Clara had finished, Bumper bent down and licked her hand. She stroked his head and he thumped his tail on the bedspread.

"I wouldn't have been so scared if you had been with me Bumper. I wish you could come everywhere with me."

Bumper let out another of his big, heavy sighs as if he agreed completely with Clara. He put his head down and curled up into a little ball. Clara and Bumper finally fell asleep and had dreams of playing soccer.

"Is everything all right Clara?" said Mrs. Grover.

"Yes, thank you," I replied.

"Good game. They sure know how to teach soccer in Chicago!"

"Thank you." I deliberately didn't look at Jessica, Harriet, and Christie, but I did glance at Mary-Lou and she smiled at me.

Bumper feels scared.

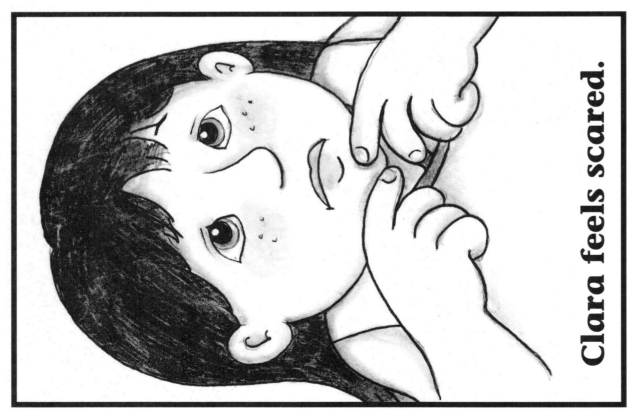

Clara feels scared.

Scared

When your heart is a' thumping
And your knee caps are a' jumping
And your voice is so wobbly, you can't speak
Then there must be something scary
Could be a spider, big and hairy
Or a monster in the closet – don't dare peek!

When your tummy feels all squirmy
And your hands cannot grip firmly
'Cause they're sweaty and their shaking to and fro
Your body's saying it's afraid
A thumping, shaking, fear parade
If you can run, you'd better do it quick and go!

Scared Puppet Patterns

Directions: Copy the scared puppet patterns for each student. The children should color them and then cut out the pieces. Punch holes where indicated and use brads to attach the arms and legs.

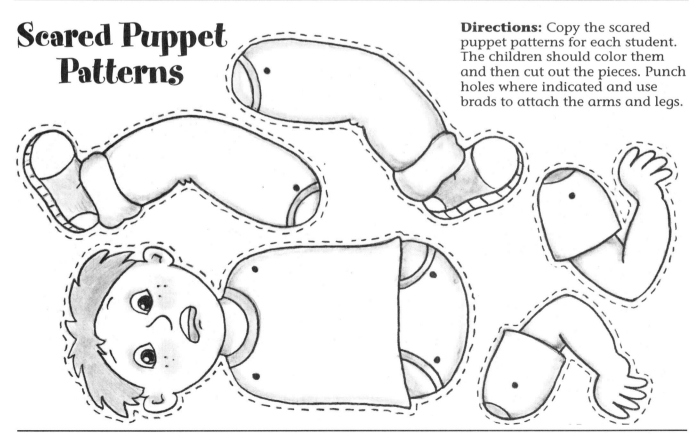

When Something Scares You - What Should You Do?

Directions: Discuss each of the illustrations with the children.
Encourage the children to take this page home and share it with their parents.

1. Talk to a teacher.

2. Talk to a parent.

3. Talk to a grandparent.

4. Talk to a trusted adult.

What's Behind the Door?

Directions: Copy this page for each student. Have the children color the door, cut it out, and fold along the dotted line. Glue the edge of the door to a piece of construction paper. The children should then draw something "scary" behind the door.

Chapter Three: Teacher's Guide
The Emotion: Jealousy

A. Before The Story

Prepare the **Emotion Picture Cards** found on page 40 according to the directions on page 5. Show the cards to the children and discuss how Clara and Bumper are feeling. Here are some guided questions:
1. How do you think Clara and Bumper are feeling in these pictures? Jealousy is a hard emotion to represent visually and it might look like other feelings. *(See, After the Story, Discussion Time, #2).*
2. How can you tell they are feeling jealous?
3. Have you ever felt jealous? What or who were you jealous of?
4. Have you ever heard the saying "green with jealousy?" What do you think that means?
5. What do you think has happened that is making Clara and Bumper feel jealous? Let's read the story and find out!

B. Read The Story

Reproduce the **Read-to-Me Story 3: *Jealous*** found on pages 33–39. Make the storybooks according to the directions on page 5. Read the story to the children. Stop and discuss each page. To retell the story as a visual presentation, prepare the character and scenery patterns found on pages 91 through 96. Directions for making the patterns are found on page 5.

C. After The Story

Comprehension Questions:
1. How does Bumper tell Clara that he wants her to continue rubbing his tummy?
2. What did Bumper do to embarrass Clara when she met Hannah?
3. Who was Clara surprised to see arrive at Hannah's house?
4. Why did Clara feel jealous?
5. Why was Bumper jealous?

Discussion Time
1. Have any of you ever felt jealous?
2. Discuss with the children that feeling jealous is quite complicated because it also feels like being lonely, or like you don't matter very much, and it can also make you feel angry (which is why Clara shouts at her mom.)
3. In the story, Clara is jealous of friendships, while the poem on page 41 deals with being jealous of things. It's helpful for the children to know that everyone wishes they looked slightly different, or had different possessions. Encourage them to appreciate all the good things in their lives.

D. Extension Activities

1. **Poem**. Teach the poem "Jealous" found on page 41. Copy the award, "What do you like best about you?" Have the children dictate the answer to that question. Write it down on the award, have the children color the award, and then send it home with them.
2. **If you had one wish . . . What would it be?** Reproduce page 42 and follow the directions.
3. **Jealousy Go Away!** Reproduce page 43 and follow the directions.

Read-to-Me Story 3

Jealousy

"Clara, Bumper's hairs are all over your bedspread. Have you been letting him sleep in your bed again?" asked Clara's mom as she was tucking her in. "Dogs sleep in baskets, people sleep in beds. That's the way it is young lady. Remember that."

"Good night Mom," said Clara, trying to avoid telling her Mom a deliberate lie. There was no way she was going to stop Bumper from jumping onto her bed at night.

Her mom kissed her, and on the way out she bent down to stroke Bumper, who was lying in his basket in the corner of Clara's bedroom.

Chapter 3: Jealousy -A-

"Good night, lovely boy," she said, "You stay in your basket, do you hear me?" Bumper's eyebrows wiggled and he glanced over at Clara, with what looked like a guilty expression on his face. Clara's Mom laughed, "If I didn't know better, I'd think he understands every word we say." She closed the door behind her.

Bumper was out of the basket and up on the bed before Clara's mom had reached the bottom stair.

"You know what I think Bumper?" Clara said, stroking his smooth silky fur. "I think Mom's a bit jealous of us because we're best friends. When I was little I always wanted to get into bed with my Mom and Dad, but since you've come, I would rather stay with you."

Chapter 3: Jealousy -B-

"Actually, I have to tell you Bumper," Clara said, still rubbing his tummy, but looking at her Beanie Babies, "Feeling jealous is the pits." Clara wiggled further down under her bedspread while still keeping a hand on Bumper's golden coat.

"I felt jealous today when we were walking down the street, but I don't think you noticed because you were too busy sniffing bushes. It's OK Bumper, that's what all dogs do when they go for a walk, and I know that. But I should tell you about it now, because if you want to know what it's like to be human, you really need to know about how it feels to be jealous."

Bumper laid his head on Clara's tummy as she continued.

Clara's room was a perfect square and was painted lilac. Along one of the walls, sitting in a neat line on the cream carpet, were Clara's Beanie Babies.

"Come to think of it Bumper, maybe my Beanie Babies are jealous of you, too. I haven't played with them at all since you came. You're so much more fun than any of them."

Bumper sniffed Clara's face and gave her a lick. She pushed him over onto his back and rubbed his tummy. He made his funny groaning noise to show how much he liked it. When she stopped, Bumper kicked his back leg in the air until Clara started rubbing his tummy again.

There aren't many kids in our neighborhood Bumper. You should be pleased about that, because that's why Mom and Dad bought you for me, so I could have some company. Anyway, when we were walking down Baldwin Avenue, and we passed that enormous brick house with the green shutters, I'd never seen anyone come in or out of that house before. If you peep into their back yard, I think you can see a trampoline, but I can't be sure. Even if that's what it is, it could be that the people who live there are old, and it's there for when the grandchildren come to visit.

Chapter 3: Jealousy -E-

So as we were walking past the door, it opened and a girl my age came out. Do you remember, Bumper? You definitely saw her because you looked up when you heard the door open. I smiled and she smiled back. I said "hi" and she said "hi" back.

"I'm new here," I said, "I live on the next block, in the house with the red door. My name is Clara."

She stood in the doorway, "Hi Clara, I'm Hannah," she said with a friendly look on her face. Then, Bumper, I'm afraid that you embarrassed me a bit, because you walked right up to the shrub next to her front door and lifted your leg and, well, you sprinkled on it.

Chapter 3: Jealousy -F-

The back door opened and Hannah's friend got out. They hugged each other and jumped up and down. When they stopped hugging, and I saw who the friend was, I couldn't believe it. It was Mary-Lou Hammerton — the girl who wants to be friends with me at school. That gave me two surprises; the first surprise was that I knew Hannah's friend, and the second surprise was that I had never imagined that Mary-Lou had friends who would be so pleased to see her.

"That's Bumper, he's my dog," I said. "Sorry about that, he's just a puppy." Hannah laughed and then we both laughed, so it really didn't matter (but I'd rather you didn't do it again Bumper, it might not be funny a second time).

"You should come over and play," she said.

"Now?" I said.

"Sorry, I can't play now because my friend is coming over." At that moment, a car pulled up behind me, and I could see from the huge smile on Hannah's face that she was really pleased to see this friend.

"Maybe later this week," she said, before running past me to the waiting car.

to plan our joint birthday party. We were born on the same day. Our moms met in the hospital when they were having us. We have always shared our birthday party."

"OK, that's fine. Bye then." I called your name Bumper, and you came running from the next door's yard, "Come on Bumper," I said, and we walked back home.

Mom asked me if I wanted a drink. I snapped at her and told her to stop bugging me. I didn't want to be with Mom, I wanted to be with Hannah and Mary-Lou.

Mary-Lou looked round.

"Hi Clara," she said, "What are you doing here?"

"I live on the next block. Why don't you both come over and play at my house?" They looked at each other, and their smiles went away and I knew right away that they were going to say no.

And I know you remember the next thing Bumper, because you got upset and barked at me. I went into the kitchen and shouted at Mom, "I hate Richmond. Why did you make me leave all my friends? You and Dad are mean. I wish you'd never made us move."

"Clara, whatever's happened?" her mom said and came towards me with her arms out to give me a hug. But I didn't want a hug, so I ran out into the backyard and sat on the swing. I was crying.

It felt horrible Bumper, knowing they were nearby, being excited and happy about their birthday party. That's what 'jealous' is Bumper, and it's a horrible feeling that makes you feel very unimportant and not very nice. I was jealous that their moms had met in the hospital and were still friends and still living in the same city. I had friends I'd known since I was a baby, but they were all in Chicago. What good were they to me now?

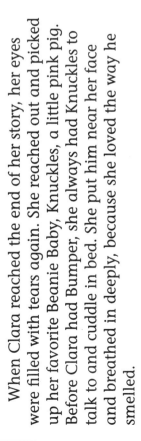

Bumper looked up and saw her holding the little pink pig. He sat up and watched for a minute. Then he nudged it with his nose, and then again, only more strongly, causing Knuckles to fly out of Clara's hands and land on the floor. Bumper leaned over the edge of the bed to look at the Beanie Baby on the carpet. He gave a little growl and then settled back next to Clara.

Clara smiled. "Maybe you do know about being jealous after all," she said to Bumper.

When Clara reached the end of her story, her eyes were filled with tears again. She reached out and picked up her favorite Beanie Baby, Knuckles, a little pink pig. Before Clara had Bumper, she always had Knuckles to talk to and cuddle in bed. She put him near her face and breathed in deeply, because she loved the way he smelled.

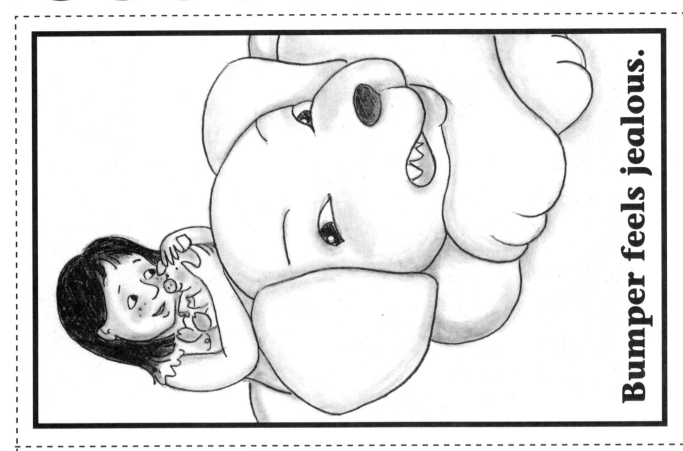

Bumper feels jealous.

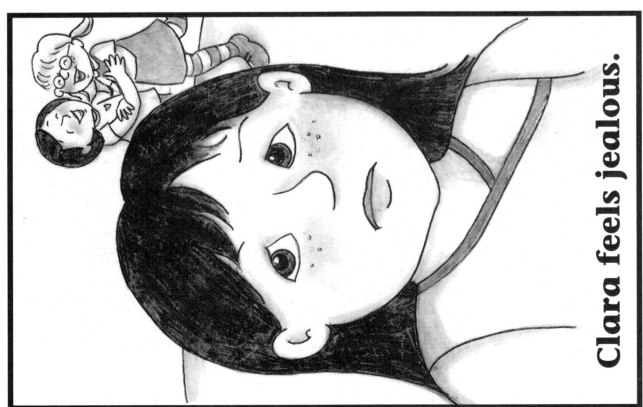

Clara feels jealous.

Happy, Sad, Jealous, Mad

Jealous

I wish my hair was longer
I wish my arms were stronger
I wish my nose was straight and not so long
I wish my bike was newer
I wish my eyes were bluer
I wish my voice could sing a nicer song.

I wish I had Ben's brother
I wish I had Beth's mother
I wish I had Carl's bedroom, it's so big
I wish I had Jane's bouncy ball
I wish I had Jack's waterfall
I wish I had a black pot bellied pig.

I wish my name was Damien
I wish I was an alien
I wish I could eat candy all day long
I wish I was a superman
I wish I had a glamorous gran
I wish I could be right and never be wrong.

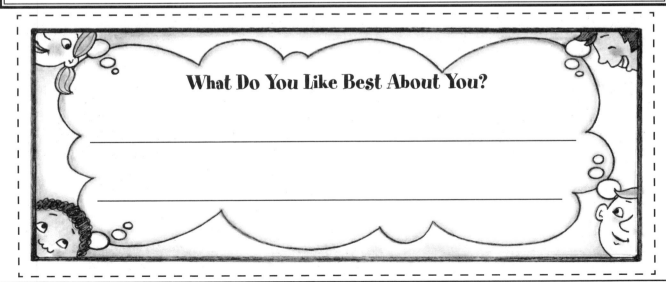

What Do You Like Best About You?

Name _____

If you had one wish . . . what would it be?

Directions: Draw a picture of your wish.

Name _____

Jealousy Go Away!

Directions: Sometimes feelings of jealousy go away when we remember some of the special things that we already have. Draw a picture of four of your special things.

1.

This is my special . . .

2. *This is my special . . .*

3.

This is my special . . .

4. *This is my special . . .*

Chapter Four: Teacher's Guide
The Emotion: Anger

A. Before The Story

Prepare the **Emotion Picture Cards** found on page 52 according to the directions on page 5. Show the cards to the children and discuss how Clara and Bumper are feeling. Here are some guided questions:

1. How do you think Clara and Bumper are feeling in these pictures?
2. How can you tell they are angry?
3. What are some things that make you feel angry?
4. How does your body feel when you are angry?
5. What do you think has happened that is making Clara and Bumper feel angry? Let's read the story and find out!

B. Read The Story

Reproduce the **Read-to-Me Story 4: Anger** found on pages 45–51. Make the storybooks according to the directions on page 5. Read the story to the children. Stop and discuss each page. To retell the story as a visual presentation, prepare the character and scenery patterns found on pages 91 through 96. Directions for making the patterns are found on page 5.

C. After The Story

Comprehension Questions:
1. How did Clara's parents know that Clara didn't have a good time on the trip?
2. Why does Clara love feeding different animals?
3. What were the two unkind things that Ben Hoyle did to Clara?
4. Why does Clara think her tears were "hot?"
5. What made Clara feel better at the end of the story?

Discussion Time
1. Why do you think losing your temper can be a little scary?
2. Can any of you think of a time when you got really angry?
3. What are some of the things we can do when we are angry to help us calm down? (See the poem on page 53.)

D. Extension Activities

1. **Poem**. Teach the poem "Angry" found on page 53. Brainstorm a list of things that make the children feel angry. Brainstorm another list of all the things that you can do to help the anger go away. Directions are found on page 53.
2. **Do You Feel Angry?** Reproduce page 54 and follow the directions.
3. **Good and Bad Ways to Get Angry**. Reproduce page 55 and follow the directions.

Read-to-Me Story 4

Angry

"How was the school field trip?" asked Clara's dad. He was late getting home from work and came straight up to Clara's bedroom to say good-night.

"Fine," said Clara. Clara's dad knew that when Clara said, 'Fine' like that, it wasn't fine at all. When she said 'Fine' like that, it meant that something had gone wrong and that she didn't want to talk about it.

When she said 'Fine' like that, her mom and dad worried and wanted to ask her what was the matter. However, they have learned it is best to leave Clara alone and hope that in a little while she would feel more like talking.

Chapter 4: Angry -A-

Clara's dad kissed her good-night and went downstairs to the kitchen where Clara's mom was writing a letter.

"What's wrong with Clara?" he asked. "I got the feeling she didn't have such a good time on the school field trip."

"I got the same feeling," said Clara's mom, closing down the computer, "but she wouldn't tell me what had happened. I wish she'd realize that it helps to talk about these things. It worries me when she bottles it all up."

What they didn't know, as they were chatting and worrying about Clara, was that at that very moment she was doing exactly what they wanted her to — talking about all her troubles.

Chapter 4: Angry -B-

"I lost my temper, Bumper. It's a bad feeling. Do you want to know what happened?" Bumper thumped his tail on the bedspread and then laid his head back down on his paws.

My class went on a field trip today. I'd been looking forward to it because I get tired of being in the classroom every day. We went to Maymont. It's a park with an old, beautiful house and lovely gardens. And there are animals, like bison, foxes, deer, and bobcats. They even have two bears, but we didn't get to see them. Greg, our guide, said they must be hiding.

"Do dogs get angry, Bumper? I know you growl and bark, but maybe that's because you're afraid. I'll tell you what Bumper, being really angry is kind of scary. It's as if you become a different person — a person who does crazy things — and afterwards when you have calmed down, you can't believe what you did."

Bumper was resting his golden head on his paws, but he looked up and gently sniffed at Clara, as if to say, "Why? What did you do?" Then he licked her cheek, "It can't be that bad," Clara was sure he was saying.

I love feeding animals because they always look so pleased to see you. It's so funny to watch the ways that different animals pick up the food and gobble it down. Goats have this way of moving their jaws in a big circle when they chew. They always make me laugh.

All the children in my class bought bags of feed pellets from the little store, and then we had to stand behind Greg who was going to tell us about safety before we started feeding the animals. I wanted to make sure I was the first one to get to the fence once Greg has finished, so I stood right in front of him.

One thing you will find out from this story Bumper, is that human boys are stupid, absolutely stupid. They don't know how to behave and they think things are funny, when they really are not. You should be glad that you're my dog Bumper, and not some stupid boy's!

Anyway, when the bus arrived at the Maymont, Greg met us and showed us round the Italian and Japanese gardens. It was very interesting! I walked with Harriet, Jessica, and Christie (the ones I want to be friends with), but the part I was looking forward to the most was buying a bag of feed pellets and being able to feed the farm animals: the donkeys, the goats, the chickens, and the rabbits.

"It was all his fault!" I pointed at him and shouted in a very loud and angry voice.

"Clara! Come and stand by me at once!" Mrs. Grover said in her strictest voice.

"But I didn't do anything!" said Clara.

"Clara, you'll be sitting on the bus if you don't calm down," replied Mrs. Grover.

I went and stood next to Mrs. Grover. It was the angriest I have ever been, Bumper. My whole body felt as if it was going to burst. I think that's why I shouted so loud —it was like an explosion was happening inside my body. I was breathing fast, just like I'd run up a hill. I was crying too, but they weren't sad tears, they were hot as if they were heated up from all the fire inside me.

"Now," Greg said, "I don't want anyone to throw any food in with the animals until I say so." He was smiling, but his voice sounded very firm. "Does everyone understand?" he asked. We all nodded. He turned around to call the goat from the other side of the field. Then stupid, stupid, stupid Ben Hoyle who was right behind me, deliberately knocked my elbow so that all the food pellets flew out of my hand. Some of them fell on the floor, but most of them hit Greg on the back!

Greg turned around and saw my empty bag of food, and in a cross voice asked, "What did you do that for?" I looked around at Ben, but he was looking as though he hadn't done anything.

I ran over to Ben and knocked the feed pellets out of his hand, just like he had done to me. Then I snatched the camera away from Ryan, dropped the camera in the mud, and jumped on it. I stamped so hard with my heels that the camera cracked in the grass. All the time I was doing this, I was shouting "I hate you! I hate you! I hate you!"

Mrs. Grover grabbed my hand and walked and walked with me until we reached a bench a long way away from everyone else. I sat down and Mrs. Grover knelt down in front of me. Her face wasn't angry she looked worried.

You wouldn't think things could get much worse, would you Bumper? But they did. Mrs. Grover was bending down to tie someone's shoelace, and Ben pointed at me and whispered something to his friend Ryan. Ryan laughed and then got his disposable camera out of his pocket and took a picture of me, with my red face and teary eyes, in trouble with Mrs. Grover.

I didn't care that Mrs. Grover could see, I didn't care that Greg would be cross with me, and I didn't care that I was sure to be punished. It was as if Clara Clapton wasn't there anymore, just a big piece of anger that looked like me.

So I had to sit all by myself with Mr. Parker, our bus driver, until the others came back. I didn't want them to come back. I thought they'd laugh at me, especially Ben Hoyle. But when he got on the bus he didn't look at me, and his eyes looked a bit red. I think he might have been crying too. That surprised me.

I stared out of the window and pretended that I didn't care that I was sitting by myself. Then I felt the seat next to me bump down. I turned and saw that Mary-Lou Hammerton was sitting next to me.

I tried to explain why I was so angry, but it was hard to talk with the big gulpy tears. My voice sounded kind of strangled. Mrs. Grover was very patient. She didn't try to hurry me and she kept her hands on my arms.

"What Ben did was very unkind Clara, but that doesn't mean what you did was OK. Can you see that? If you had stayed calm and told me or Greg what had happened, you wouldn't be in trouble now," Mrs. Grover explained.

She stood up, "I'm afraid you're going to have to sit on the bus until the others get back. You can read a book if you like."

         Happy, Sad, Jealous, Mad

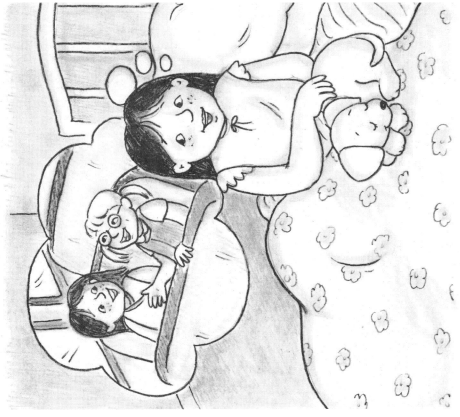

Then we laughed and I felt a little bit better.

So Bumper, now I know two things. I know what it feels like to really lose my temper, and I know I've got to try and control it. Clara looked at Bumper and saw that he had fallen asleep. Even in his sleep Bumper appeared to have a smile on his face. She kissed the top of his head and then laid back down. Sometimes I still wish I was a dog, she thought as she fell asleep.

"Last year I got so angry," she said in a quiet voice so no one else could hear.

"I was so sure I was going to win the race during Track and Field Day, that when I came in third instead, I lost my temper so badly, I had to stay in at recess for a whole week."

"What did you do?" I asked. "It can't be as bad as what I did."

"Oh, yes it can. It was worse," said Mary-Lou. "What? Tell me. What did you do?" I asked.

"I laid down on the track, kicked my feet, thumped my fists on the ground, and when Mrs. MacDonald, my teacher, tried to pick me up, I bit her! My mom said she had never been so embarrassed in her whole life," said Mary-Lou.

Bumper feels angry.

Clara feels angry.

Angry

I'm like a human volcano
I bubble and hiss inside
My anger is hot, and do you know what?
You might just want to hide.

There's steam coming out of my ears
There's a stomp coming out of my feet
I'll scream and shout, so you're in no doubt
That I'm angry, and you'll all feel the heat.

I might go and punch a pillow
I might go and shout at the cat
I might count to ten, scribble pictures in felt pen
I might jump, or hit balls with a bat.

Then the fire will start to die down
And the heat will cool in a while
The steam from my ears, the shouts and angry tears
Will be gone, and if you're lucky, I will smile.

Brainstorm

Directions: Have the children brainstorm a list of all the things that make them angry.

Then discuss different "peaceful" ways that the children could use to resolve those situations.

Name _____

Do You Feel Angry?

Directions: Talk about each picture with the students. Color either the "happy" or the "sad" face.

Good and Bad Ways to Get Angry

Directions: Discuss with the children how it feels to be angry. Have the children color the pictures that show appropriate ways to show anger. Put an "X" on the inappropriate ways to show anger.

Chapter Five: Teacher's Guide
The Emotion: Embarrassed

A. Before The Story

Prepare the **Emotion Picture Cards** found on page 64 according to the directions on page 5. Show the cards to the children and discuss how Clara and Bumper are feeling. Here are some guided questions:

1. How do you think Clara and Bumper are feeling in these pictures?
2. They are feeling embarrassed. Can anyone tell the class what "being embarrassed" means? *(This is a difficult concept for children to describe. Help them by relating examples of moments when you have felt embarrassed.)*
3. Have any of you ever felt embarrassed? Does anyone want to share an embarrassing story?
4. What do you think has happened that is making Clara and Bumper feel embarrassed? Let's read the story and find out!

B. Read The Story

Reproduce the **Read-to-Me Story 5: *Embarrassed*** found on pages 57–63. Make the storybooks according to the directions on page 5. Read the story to the children. Stop and discuss each page. To retell the story as a visual presentation, prepare the character and scenery patterns found on pages 91 through 96. Directions for making the patterns are on page 5.

C. After The Story

Comprehension Questions:
1. Why was Bumper so tired at the beginning of the story?
2. Why does Clara think being embarrassed wouldn't be as bad for dogs as it is for humans?
3. What sort of dancing did the class have to do for assembly?
4. What did Clara do that was so embarrassing?
5. What makes Clara think that all boys might not be stupid after all?

Discussion Time
1. Does anyone want to tell us their most embarrassing moment? (For adults and children it is a huge relief to share these stories. The children would love to hear their teacher's most embarrassing moment.)
2. If you are embarrassed, what do you think is the best way of handling it?
3. If someone else is embarrassed, how can you make them feel better?

D. Extension Activities

1. **Poem**. Teach the poem "Embarrassed" found on page 65. Copy the frame at the bottom of the page for each child. To make a mirror, have the children color the frame and then glue a piece of aluminum foil in the center.
2. **Embarrassing Moments!** Reproduce page 66 and follow the directions.
3. **Embarrassment Bear**. Reproduce page 67 and follow the directions.

Read-to-Me Story 5

Embarrassed

"Bumper, wake up!" Clara whispered as loudly as she could across her dark bedroom. The puppy was in a deep sleep and Clara could hear him breathing in and out, in and out.

Clara and Bumper had been playing all evening in the backyard by chasing fireflies and putting them in glass jars. Bumper didn't know what to make of these strange little creatures and he barked at them every time they glowed in the twilight. Now he was worn out and had fallen asleep earlier than usual. But Clara still wanted to talk to him.

She jumped out of bed and ran across the thick carpet to his basket. She gently lifted one of his silky ears and whispered, "Wake up Bumper." Bumper opened his eyes and lifted his head immediately. Yawning, he sat up and wagged his tail at Clara.

"You can't sleep yet Bumper. You know we only pretend to Mom and Dad that you sleep in your basket, but you really sleep with me on my bed. And anyway, I've got something else important to teach you about what it's like to be human," Clara said to Bumper.

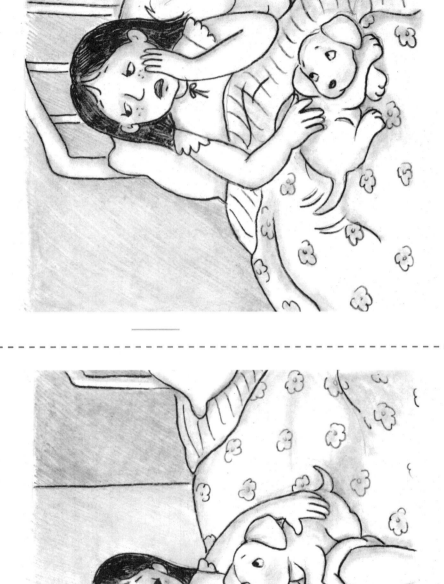

"I don't think dogs know what this feeling is like Bumper, but even if you do, it can't possibly be as bad for you. Want to know why?" Bumper thumped his tail on Clara's legs that were stretched out under the blankets."

"It's because you have fur, and that means you can't blush," she said, petting his back. "Blushing is what happens when you get this dreadful thing I'm going to tell you about. When you blush, everyone knows exactly how you are feeling inside, and you can't hide it. This feeling is called embarrassment."

Chapter 5: Embarrassed -D-

She walked back to her bed. Bumper stood up, stretched both of his back legs in turn, and then he jumped up on the bed next to her.

"What you need to know about being human," Clara said sitting up in bed, with her arm round her dog, "is a terrible, dreadful feeling that people have sometimes. I think it's worse than being afraid, or worse than falling over and making your knees bleed." Bumper was watching Clara closely now, as if he was anxious to find out what this awful thing was.

Chapter 5: Embarrassed -C-

Bumper made a little groaning noise and lifted his paws up and down on the bed. "Do you want me to get on with the story Bumper?" Bumper smacked his mouth and swallowed loudly, "All right then, but you must promise not to laugh at me," instructed Clara.

Mrs. Grover was asking for trouble, if you ask me, by making us do a dance for a class assembly. Not one single boy wanted to do it, and although the girls don't mind dancing, they did mind when Mrs. Grover said that we had to dance with the boys, and that we had to hold hands!

"I had felt embarrassed before, like when I held hands with this stranger at the food store because I thought that person was my mom. Or when I told Beth that I didn't like Denna's new sweater and Denna was standing right behind me. But those times were nothing compared to how I felt today. I can hardly bear to tell you Bumper, because the thing about embarrassment is that you feel it all over again when you remember it. My mom says the feeling can even come back years afterwards."

"Come on, boys," Mrs. Grover kept saying, when they refused to hold hands with us, "girls aren't poisonous."

Anyway, even though I didn't like having to dance with Ben, we were quite good at it. We always skipped in time to the music and we knew which way we were supposed to be going, which is more than can be said of most of the others. All week Mrs. Grover has been shouting over the music, "Watch Ben and Clara everyone, watch what they do and follow them."

Being good at country dancing made it a bit more fun, and sometimes I even forgot I was holding Ben's hands, because I was concentrating so hard on the dancing.

Mrs. Grover is from England and she says that children in England do this sort of dancing all the time. It's called country dancing, and you have to skip around in time to the music while holding hands with your dance partner. Every now and then you have to stand face to face and make an arch for other people to skip under. It's more complicated than that Bumper, but I don't think you'd understand. But just think how awful it has been to spend all week practicing this dance while holding horrid, stupid Ben Hoyle's hands.

Then the music started and Ben and I counted to six, and then we skipped our way into the auditorium and up onto the stage, with everyone else following us. We skipped from the back to the front, and we were moving quite fast. But just as Ben turned left and I turned right, my heel slipped out from under me! I shot off the stage and fell right into the front row where the first grade children were sitting.

Ben stopped and stared down at me, and as each pair skipped to the front and saw me sprawled on the floor, they forgot to go to the left or right. They just stopped and stared down at me!

This morning the whole school was watching us in the hall. The janitor had set up the auditorium so everyone had a good view of us. Mrs. Grover was standing at the back next to the sound system so she could turn the music on.

We were all lined up by the door. Mrs. Grover had told us that when the music started, we must count to six in time to the music, and then Ben and I had to start skipping into the auditorium, then skip up the steps and onto the stage. Then we were going to skip in pairs from the back of the stage to the very front and when each pair got to the front, the boys were supposed to turn left, and the girls were supposed to turn right.

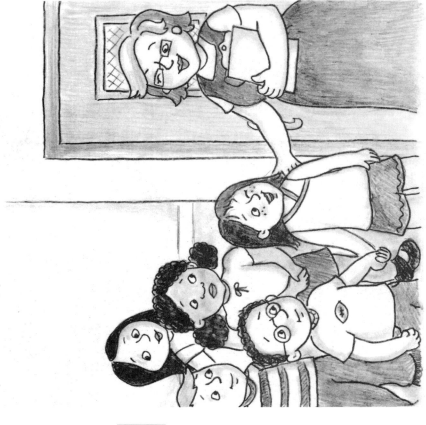

People were still laughing and my face was still red, but what she said made me feel brave. Mrs. Grover turned to face the school. She clapped her hands, and said, "Sorry about that everyone. We'll start again. Class, please line up outside."

She click clicked her way to the back of the hall again in her high heels. Once she was next to the sound system, she caught my eye and winked. Then I wanted to do it again, just for her.

Mrs. Grover turned the music off and for a second there was silence. Then someone started to laugh and then someone else, and before long everyone on the stage and everyone in the audience was laughing – at me!

I stood up but I didn't know what to do next. My face felt as if it had been painted with liquid fire. I knew I was bright red. Mrs. Grover came and asked me if I was alright. I nodded, but I wanted to run away and never come back. She leaned in close to my ear and whispered, "Come on Clara, this happens to good dancers all the time. Now hold your head high, and we'll do it again."

Everyone laughed again and I felt my face warming up. Mrs. Grover told Ryan not to be unkind and that I had been very brave to get back up and start the dance again. (That's the other bad thing about being embarrassed Bumper, people like to remind you of it.)

You'll never guess what happened next Bumper, Ben Hoyle shouted over to Ryan, "She's a better dancer than you, any day," which made me realize that not all boys are stupid all of the time.

This time I didn't slip. During the second dance everyone started clapping in time to the music, and not one of us made a single mistake. In class afterwards, Mrs. Grover smiled more than she usually does and said she thought we had done really well, and that we had made her very proud.

Ryan Bywater put up his hand and asked Mrs. Grover if everyone could fly into the audience next time like Clara, because the audience seemed to like that part the best.

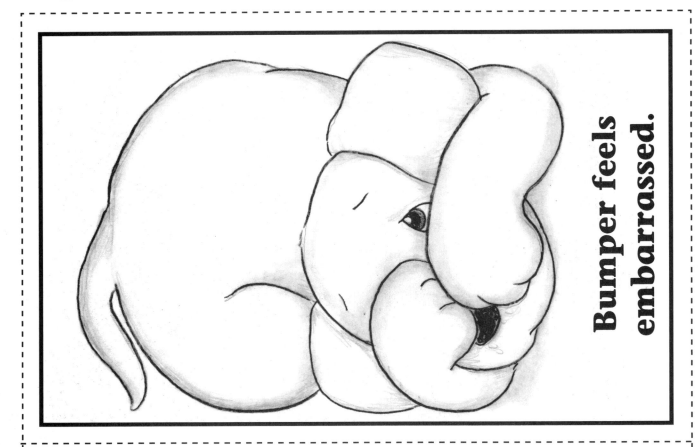

Bumper feels embarrassed.

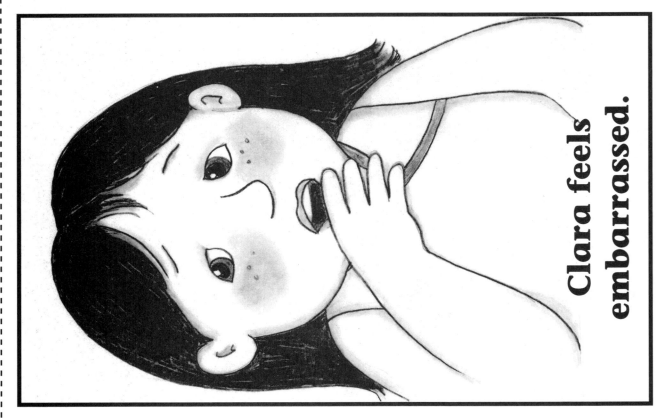

Clara feels embarrassed.

Embarrassed

I feel so silly, I don't want to go red
I wish I could vanish, or hide under my bed
Everyone's laughing, they think it's such fun
To see me embarrassed, at what I have done.

I want to hide, to run far away
But I have to stand here, I have to stay
My friends think it's funny, I think it's not -
It's hard to look cool, when your face is so hot!

I'll wait a while, 'til my face doesn't glow
I'll try to be calm, for there's one thing I know
Today, I'm embarrassed, it makes my face burn
But don't laugh too hard, next it might be your turn!

Directions: Color and cut out the frame. Glue a piece of aluminum foil in the center. Look in the mirror. Has your face ever turned red?

Embarrassing Moments!

Directions: Discuss the events below and stress these are things that happen to everyone!

Embarrassment Bear

Directions: Copy the pattern onto card stock, color, cut-out, and attach the arms with brads.

We all feel embarrassed from time to time. Sometimes when we are embarrassed we want to hide. Cover the bear's face with his paws to show that he is embarrassed. Help him feel better and move his arms back down.

Chapter Six: Teacher's Guide
The Emotion: Sad

A. Before The Story

Prepare the **Emotion Picture Cards** on page 76 according to the directions on page 5. Show the cards to the children and discuss how Clara and Bumper are feeling. Here are some guided questions:

1. How do you think Clara and Bumper are feeling in these pictures?
2. How can you tell they are feeling sad?
3. Can all of you make a "sad face?" What does a face look like when it is "sad?"
4. What do you think has happened that is making Clara and Bumper feel sad? Let's read the story and find out!

B. Read The Story

Reproduce the **Read-to-Me Story 6: Sad** found on pages 69–75. Make the storybooks according to the directions on page 5. Read the story to the children. Stop and discuss each page. To retell the story as a visual presentation, prepare the character and scenery patterns found on pages 91 through 96. Directions for making the patterns are found on page 5.

C. After The Story

Comprehension Questions:
1. What did Clara normally do when she received a letter from Chicago?
2. What was the sad news in the letter?
3. What were some of the things Clara and her parents remembered about Grandpa Denna?
4. What made Clara and her parents laugh?
5. Why didn't Clara feel she needed to tell Bumper about her sadness?

Discussion Time
1. Why do you think we cry when we're sad?
2. Imagine if our bodies were different and when we were sad, something else happened *(think of some funny examples, e.g., our hair stood up on end, or our ears wiggled)*. Encourage the children to come up with their own ideas.
3. What helps you when you are sad? How can we help others when they are sad?

D. Extension Activities

1. **Poem**. Teach the poem "Sad" found on page 77. Copy the "Happy Gram" found at the bottom of the page for each child. The children should decorate their "Happy Grams" with crayons and glitter. Explain to the children that they should save their "Happy Grams" until they see someone who is feeling sad. Then give the Happy Gram to the person who is sad in order to cheer them up.
2. **Everyone Feels Sad Sometimes**. Reproduce page 78 and follow the directions.
3. **Help These Kids Feel Better**. Reproduce page 79 and follow the directions.

Sad

Clara's mom was kneeling on the kitchen floor playing with Bumper. "You're such a clever dog," she was saying to him as Clara came in from school.

"Why, what's he done?" Clara asked, laughing as the excited dog slid on the wooden floor in his hurry to greet her.

"It's the way he moves his eyebrows and looks at you when you're talking," Clara's mom said while standing up, "he really looks like he understands."

"He does," said Clara. "He understands about being scared, and jealous, and embarrassed, and angry. He knows more about human feelings than any other dog in Richmond."

"If not the entire United States," said Clara's mother.

"If not the whole world," said Clara. They both laughed and Bumper jumped up and down and barked excited yelps.

Busy preparing the meal, Clara's mom didn't notice that Clara was still in her room a whole hour later. She had no idea that the letter from Chicago contained sad news, and that Clara was lying on her bed crying.

When Clara dropped the letter and started to cry, Bumper leapt up next to her and made little whining noises. He tried to lick her face and nudged her with his soft brown nose, but Clara's body still jerked with her tears, and she kept making a sobbing noise.

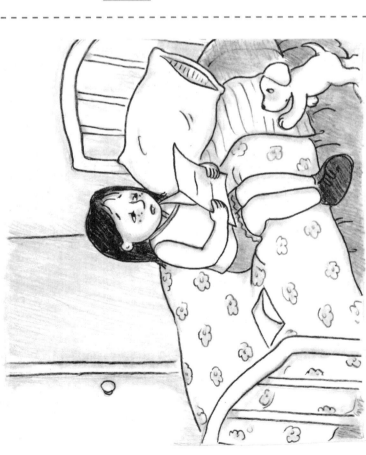

"Oh, I forgot!" said Clara's mom while sorting through a pile of mail on the kitchen counter, "you've got a letter from Chicago. I think it's from Denna."

"Great!" said Clara, taking the letter from her mother and running upstairs to her bedroom. Bumper slid on the floor again because he was hurrying so much to keep up with her.

Clara always liked to read letters from her old friends in her room, with just Bumper for company, and later she would come back downstairs and read parts of it out loud to her parents. But on this day Clara didn't come back downstairs.

She walked out the kitchen door and Bumper ran all the way to the top of the stairs. Before she was half way up the stairs, Clara's mom could hear her daughter sobbing. She ran the rest of the way to Clara's room.

"Darling, what's happened?"

Clara sat up on the bed and held her arms out to her mom in a way she hadn't done for a long time.

"It's Grandpa Denna, he's dead," she managed to say before her face dissolved into crying again.

Clara's mom listened to music as she cooked, so she didn't hear when Bumper came into the kitchen. The first she noticed Bumper was when he was batting at her feet and whining.

"Hey Bumper," she said, "What's up? Where's Clara?" When she said this, Bumper ran to the kitchen door and then turned round and looked at her.

She laughed, "What silly game are you playing with me?" But Bumper ran to the first stair step, then ran back to the kitchen door, and let out a bark.

"What is it Bumper?" She was more serious now. "Do you want me to come upstairs with you?" asked Clara's mom. Bumper barked a loud, "yes!"

At dinner, they told Clara's dad the news. Clara's face and eyes were puffy and her eyes were a little red. Every so often her body would breath in deeply, as if it was trying to catch some extra air.

"Let's all remember something good about him," said Clara's dad. "I liked the way he used to read stories to you and Denna when you were little, and he used to put Denna on one knee and you on the other."

"I liked that way he always had candy in his pocket for me," said Clara, trying to eat her food even though she wasn't hungry. "And I liked the way his sweaters smelled like lemons."

Denna's grandpa had lived with Denna's family. Clara had known him all her life and gave him the name, Grandpa Denna, when she was only two. He used to babysit for her and he spent hours playing with the girls when they were very young.

Clara's mom held her tight while she cried and cried. Bumper laid down on the floor next to the bed. "Poor Clara," said her mom after a while, "He was like a grandpa to you as well, wasn't he?" That made Clara cry all over again.

 Happy, Sad, Jealous, Mad

"I liked the way when he told jokes, he would start laughing before he got to the end. Sometimes he laughed so much, he never got to the end of the joke," said Clara's dad, "I didn't know if he was laughing or crying."

"I liked the way he made me feel safe," cried Clara.

Now all three of them were crying and poor Bumper moved from one to the other, licking their hands or putting his head on their laps.

Clara's dad got some tissues from the drawer and they all blew their noses at the same time, which made them laugh just a little.

"I liked the way he always rang our door bell when he was going to the store and asked if he could get anything for us," said Clara's mom.

"I liked the way he laughed. His eyes went all twinkly," said Clara, feeling her own eyes go watery again.

"I liked the way he would come for a cup of coffee and talk to me while I cooked dinner," Clara's mom said as her voice went a little wobbly.

"And I liked the way he put pictures I drew for him up on his bedroom wall," Clara said. She felt a gulp in her throat and knew she was going to cry again.

he feels sad because he loves us."

Later that evening, Clara took Bumper for a walk around the neighborhood. She didn't feel like playing or running, but walking with Bumper shuffling around by her side felt good.

She didn't want to go to bed that night. She didn't want to lie awake while still being sad and thinking about Grandpa Denna.

"I think we should write down all of our favorite memories of Grandpa Denna and send them to Denna and her family. It helps when someone you love dies, to know that other people loved them too," said Clara's mom.

She went over to the computer in the corner of the kitchen and quickly typed in the things they had just said. Bumper was sitting next to Clara's chair and kept looking up at her.

"Bumper knows something's wrong doesn't he?" said Clara's dad, leaning across to pat him on the head.

"I think that's because sadness is a very strong feeling," said her mom, "Even though it's invisible, Bumper knows it's there. I think he can feel it too and

Clara lay in the dark. She didn't feel like telling Bumper about her sadness, and besides, it seemed as though he already understood it.

Soon Clara heard the creaking of Bumper's basket and the sound of little paws creeping across the carpet. Softly he climbed onto her bed and lay right next to her in the dark. Every so often he would sigh a deep sigh. There was something comforting about lying there with him, not saying anything and just being sad together.

There must be some feelings, she thought to herself, that are too big for words — the way she felt about Grandpa Denna was exactly like that.

"How can I stop feeling sad?" asked Clara when her dad came to tuck her in. She felt her bottom lip wobbling again.

"You can't my love," he said. "And it's right to feel sad when something sad happens. Every time you think of Grandpa Denna, choose a happy memory of him. If you do that every time, before long, whenever he comes into your head you'll have a happy thought. It won't stop you from missing him, but it will stop you from forgetting all the wonderful things about him."

"Thanks Dad, I'll try." They kissed each other good night.

Bumper feels sad.

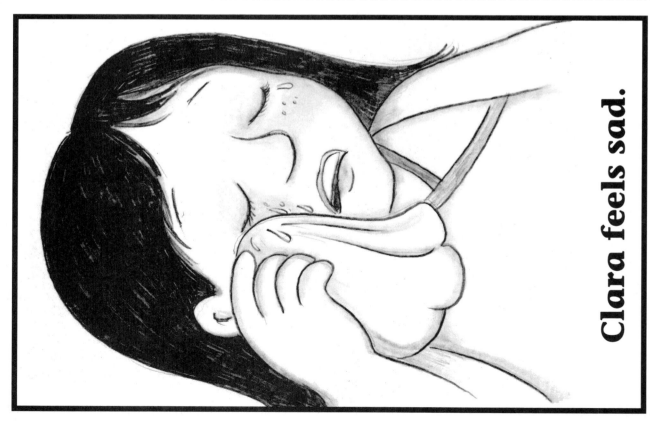

Clara feels sad.

Sad

When tears sting my eyes
And I know I'm going to cry
I wish it didn't have to be this way
If only I could dry them, soak them up or simply hide them
Forget all about them - go and play.

But when tears sting my eyes
And I know I'm going to cry
I know that it has to be this way
I need to let them flow, find somebody that I know
'I'm sad and want a hug,' I need to say.

When my eyes are dry of tears
And I've let my body weep
I blow my nose and blink my eyes a little while
I really don't know why, but once you've had a cry
You feel relieved and so much better, by a mile.

Happy Gram for: _____
Just to brighten your day!

Everyone Feels Sad Sometimes

Directions: Color each face. Use small drops of white glue to make tears. The glue will dry clear and will look like real tears.

Help These Kids Feel Better

Directions: Copy, color, and cut out the puzzle pieces. Match the puzzle pieces and glue them together on another sheet of paper.

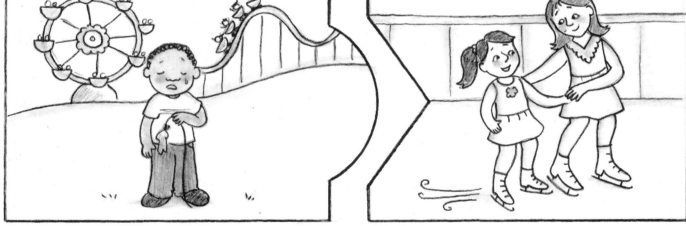

Chapter Seven: Teacher's Guide
The Emotion: Happy

A. Before The Story

Prepare the **Emotion Picture Cards** found on page 88 according to the directions on page 5. Show the cards to the children and discuss how Clara and Bumper are feeling. Here are some guided questions:
1. How do you think Clara and Bumper are feeling in these pictures?
2. How can you tell they are feeling happy?
3. What kind of things do you think make a dog feel happy?
4. Brainstorm a list of some of the things that make the children feel happy.
5. What do you think has happened that is making Clara and Bumper feel happy? Let's read the story and find out!

B. Read The Story

Reproduce the **Read-to-Me Story 7: *Happy*** found on pages 81–87. Make the storybooks according to the directions on page 5. Read the story to the children. Stop and discuss each page. To retell the story as a visual presentation, prepare the character and scenery patterns found on pages 91 through 96. Directions for making the patterns are found on page 5.

C. After The Story

Comprehension Questions:
1. Why is Clara sulking at the beginning of the story?
2. How did Mary-Lou surprise Clara when they were playing soccer?
3. Why do Mary-Lou and Clara have to sit on the sideline?
4. What is the message that Mary-Lou sends to Clara?
5. Who are Clara's two friends in Richmond?

Discussion Time
1. What do you do to show people you are sulking?
2. What do you do when you are really happy?
3. Tell us about the time when you were the happiest.

E. Extension Activities

1. **Poem**. Teach the poem "Happy" found on page 89. Copy the smiling mouth puppet pattern at the bottom of page 89 for each child. Have the children color, cut out, and tape the pattern to a craft stick. The children can move the puppet as they recite the poem.
2. **Fold Book**. Reproduce page 90 and follow the directions.
3. **Conclusion of all the stories.** This story concludes all of the stories about Clara and Bumper. Review each of the Emotion Picture Cards with the children. Talk about some of the stories. Which were some of the children's favorite stories and why.

Happy

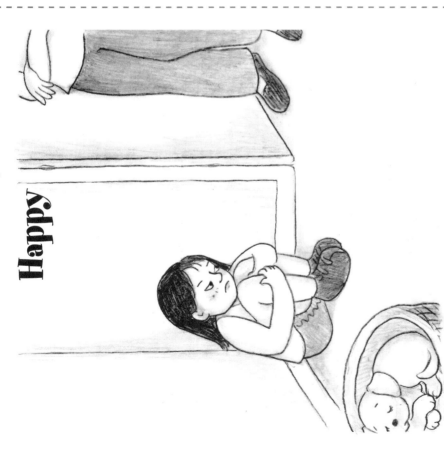

Bumper sat in his basket in the opposite corner while watching Clara, swallowing every now and then and licking his lips. An hour earlier, Clara had been happy. She was happy that she only had one week left at Richmond Elementary before the summer vacation. She had been there a whole semester! Only 7 days until the thing she had been longing for was finally going to happen.

She and her mom were going to get on an airplane and fly to Chicago. She would spend two happy weeks with Denna and Beth in the beautiful old apartment building that she used to live in. She would spend a week at Beth's and then a week at Denna's, but during the day all three of them would play together, just like they used to. Her mom would stay with her best friend, who also lived in the same apartment building.

Clara was sulking in her room. When Clara sulks this is what she does. She sits on the floor, wedged into a corner. She pulls her knees close to her chest. She scrunches her dark eyebrows close together and squeezes her red lips into a straight, angry line. Then she stares at the floor. If her mom or dad come into her room, she won't even look up. If they ask her a question, she stares even harder at the floor with her blue eyes and keeps her lips tightly shut.

 Happy, Sad, Jealous, Mad

"Clara, I'm sorry it's come as a surprise. I didn't think I needed to explain all of this to you. I just thought you'd realize that Bumper would have to stay home with Dad."

"Well I didn't!" Clara stood up from the table and clenched her fists together, "I want Denna and Beth to meet him, and I won't go without him!"

"Well, you'll have to!" said Clara's mom, who wasn't feeling very patient that day. "He's staying here with Dad and that's that."

But an hour ago everything changed. Clara had been in the kitchen with her mom and asked, "Will Bumper sit on the floor on the airplane or on his own seat?"

Clara's mom looked at her with a frown and said, "Bumper's not coming Clara, he's staying here with Dad."

Clara felt like she had been punched in the stomach. "But Bumper comes everywhere with me," said Clara.

"Think about it Clara, even if he was allowed on the airplane, you know that pets aren't allowed in the apartment building," replied Clara's mom.

"But he's not a pet – he's Bumper," cried Clara.

Happy, Sad, Jealous, Mad

Lessons were cancelled because it was the last day. People could play games that they brought in or play on the computers.

"Attention eveyone," said Mrs. Grover over the hubbub of the classroom. "Get your tennis shoes and lets go outside. We're going to play soccer."

This was the thing that Clara was best at, so she enjoyed the game, even though Harriet, Jessica, and Christie kept telling her not to show off.

When Clara lived in Chicago, Clara had never wanted a pet. She was busy and had lots of friends. She did know there was a no pets rule in her apartment building, but it had never mattered to her.

So there was nothing left for Clara to do but sulk. And sulk she did, all morning while Bumper dozed in his basket, waking up and glancing over at her every now and then. Clara promised herself that she was going to sulk until she was 18, just to show her Mom how angry she was. But when it came to the last day of school, she couldn't help secretly feeling excited and looking forward to leaving for Chicago the next day, even though she would be going without her best friend, Bumper.

"You idiot! Why don't you watch where you're going?" Clara said with her teeth clenched together.

"You watch where you're going! It was your fault too!" shouted Mary-Lou.

Clara was surprised to hear Mary-Lou talk like this. She was usually quiet and always smiled at Clara, even when she wasn't being very kind to her.

"Are you two alright?" asked Mrs. Grover, who had run over to them. "I think you should both sit on the side line for a few minutes, you might feel dizzy."

It was a close match and the other team looked like they were about to score their third goal. Clara ran as fast as she could to the goal area and managed to take the ball away from Ryan Bywater before he could score. She spun around with the ball next to her right foot, and she was getting ready to kick it to the other end of the field, but she didn't see Mary-Lou coming in from the other direction. They crashed into each other, knocked heads, and fell to the ground. The ball dribbled into the net and scored a goal for the other team.

Clara felt a strange feeling spread through her body, knowing that Mary Lou had noticed all the unkind things she had done. Because Mary Lou never said anything, Clara thought she hadn't really noticed.

"I'm sorry," Clara heard herself saying. "I think I've been angry the whole term because I wanted to be friends with . . ."

"Jessica, Harriet, and Christie, yes I know," said Mary Lou. "That's been obvious, too."

"I'm going to Chicago for two weeks, but when I get back would you like to come and play? We could invite Hannah, too."

Mary Lou smiled a big smile and Clara realized that she had never seen her smile like this before – a really happy smile.

After they got changed, Clara and Mary-Lou swapped phone numbers and promised to get in touch after Clara returned from Chicago.

So the two girls sat cross-legged next to each other. Clara snatched pieces of grass out of the ground and Mary-Lou pretended to concentrate on the match. Suddenly Mary-Lou turned around and said, "Why have you been so horrid to me, Clara Clapton? All I ever wanted was to be your friend."

"You already have a friend, the girl who lives down my street. If you wanted to be my friend, why didn't you invite me to your party?" replied Clara.

"I wanted to, but I thought if you were rude to me like you are at school, I would look stupid for having invited someone who doesn't even like me," answered Mary-Lou.

The taxi ride from the airport to the center of Chicago went very quickly. Clara's nose was pressed against the window the whole time, looking at all the sights that used to be so familiar. When they pulled up outside the building that had been home for six years, Clara felt like crying again but she wasn't sure why.

They buzzed the intercom to Denna's apartment as they had agreed. Denna and Beth's voices squealed out into the street and there was a clunk as the door unlocked.

Beth, Denna, and Clara jumped up and down and hugged and shrieked in the way that some young girls do when they are very happy. Clara's mom reached into her bag to answer her phone and then went into the apartment to talk to Clara's dad.

Clara stopped sulking around her Mom when she got home that night, and they had fun packing her suitcase together. But saying goodbye to Bumper at the airport was dreadful, she cried so much when she hugged him that the fur on the top of his head was dark and wet from her tears.

"What about me?" said her Dad, trying to make Clara laugh, "Aren't you going to miss me? Don't I get any tears?" Clara smiled, but couldn't quite manage a laugh.

When Clara and her mom walked into to the airport, Bumper tried to follow and whined a little when Clara's dad picked him up.

"Try not to think about it," said her mom as they settled in their seats. "We'll be back before you know it."

"Who's Mary-Lou?" said Beth and Denna at exactly the same time, which made them all laugh again.

"She is my friend in Richmond," said Clara. This thought made Clara smile. She told her friends, "I've got two friends in Richmond, Mary-Lou and Bumper. You'd like them both. They're great."

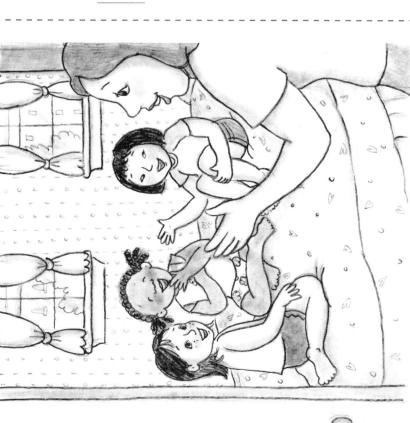

Clara went to Beth's room to put her suitcase away. The three girls sat on the bed and chatted. Then there was a knock at the door.

"You may enter," said Beth in a funny, grown-up voice that made them all laugh.

Clara's mom put her head round the door, "That was Dad on the phone, he sends his love and says that Mary-Lou called you to say that she hopes you have a great time with your friends."

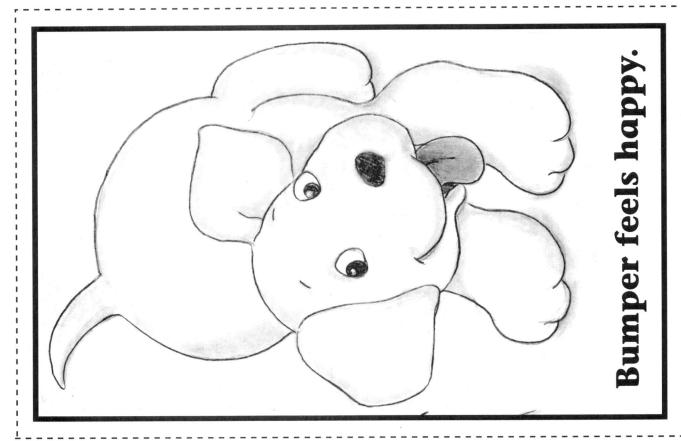

Bumper feels happy.

Clara feels happy.

Happy

My lips stretch out into a great big smile
My eyes shine and twinkle, and sparkle for a while
I can't stand still, or sit in a chair
I jump up and down, wave my hands in the air
Laughter bubbles up from deep below
And bursts out my mouth, with a yo ho ho.
I dance a silly dance and I sing a silly song
I think I'd get worn out if I was happy all day long.

Smiling Mouth Puppet Pattern

Directions: Copy, color, and cut out the smiling mouth pattern. Attach it to a craft stick with glue or double-stick tape. Let the children hold the big smile as they learn the "Happy" poem.

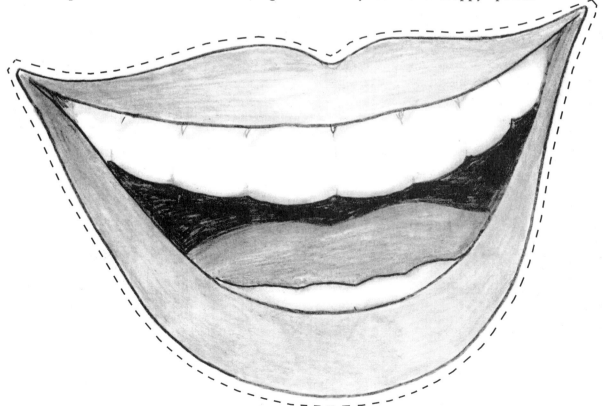

Fold Book Directions: Copy, color, and cut out along the dotted lines. Fold along the solid lines. Read together.

-3-

Bumper is happy.

-2-

Clara is happy.

They are both happy.

-4-

Being Happy!

Clara
and
Bumper

-1-

Happy, Sad, Jealous, Mad

Character Patterns

Happy Clara

Clara's Dad

Clara's Mom

Bumper

 Happy, Sad, Jealous, Mad

Scared Clara

Embarrassed Clara

Sad Clara

Angry Clara

Lonely Clara

Jealous Clara

Beth

Ryan

Christie

Ben

Mary-Lou

Harriet

Mrs. Grover

Jessica

Hannah

Happy, Sad, Jealous, Mad

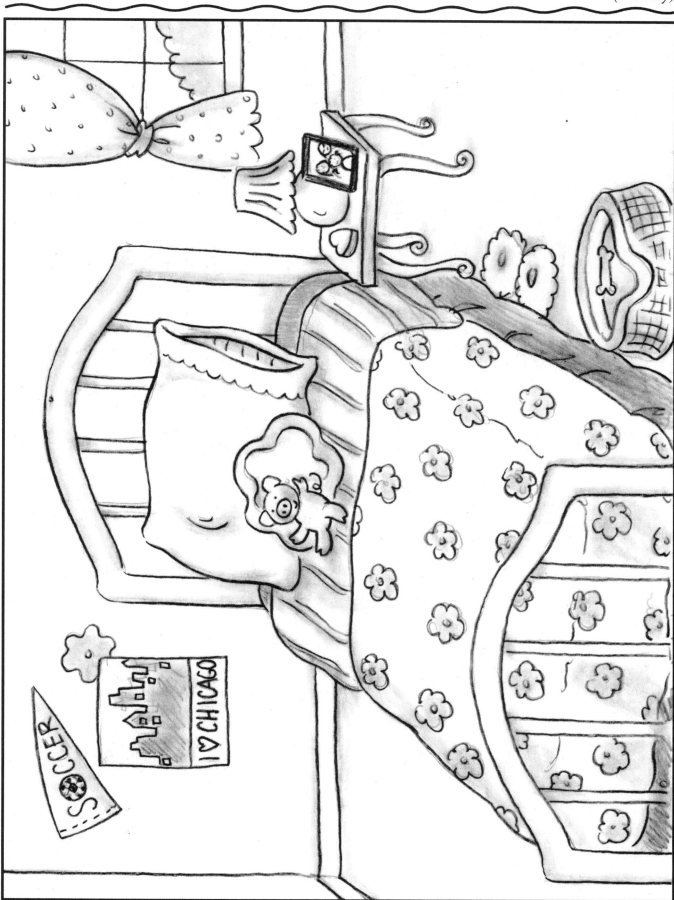